Flavours of Margaret River

Text by Michael Zekulich

Wines and Recipes from
Amberley Estate • Clairault Wines
Voyager Estate • Xanadu

Churchill Press

Margaret River

Three and a half hours drive from Perth, in Western Australia's spectacular South-West, is the busy bustling town of Margaret River, the new heartland of the state's wine industry. But little more than three decades ago it was a tiny hamlet providing basic needs for the district's struggling farmers and timber workers.

No one in those days could possibly have envisaged a community bursting with pride in its international quality wines made in unique wineries with cellar door facilities as attractive as any in the land. In their small timber cottages, often with earthen floors, they could never have foreseen the range of accommodation and stylish restaurants that would be built for an ever-increasing number of tourists from all over the world, also attracted to the stunning coastline, surfing beaches and forests that provide so much of the inspiration for the region's many arts and crafts specialists.

And even when the good wines started to flow, who would have dreamt of the entertainment that would follow, like the world renowned Leeuwin Estate alfresco concerts where internationally acclaimed orchestras and artists have brought enormous pleasure to thousands? On balmy summer nights, they pack the sweeping lawns to enjoy picnic meals, fine wines,

music and song with an unusual backing – the calls of kookaburras from the majestic surrounding karri trees. At the first concert, featuring the famous London Philharmonic Orchestra, one could sense the ghosts of the early English pioneers – starved of culture when settling in a new strange land – dancing among the trees behind the orchestral shell, celebrating the joyous sounds of the most skilful musicians of their homeland.

But Margaret River is also special for its own rich Australian heritage. Scattered about can still be found old group settlement cottages, the basic homes built by those seeking to clear the massive tall trees and farm the land. In such labours, with primitive equipment, they suffered the aching backs, the bleeding blisters and the heartache. But behind them, they left a platform of great spirit for the modern wine industry pioneers to draw strength from, and to build upon.

Today, premium Margaret River wines can be found on sale in many of the English towns and villages from whence those hardy settlers had come, perhaps to be sipped and enjoyed by their ancestors.

Said Di Cullen, who with (late) husband Kevin had bought 100 acres for 100 pounds in 1956 as a base to go fishing, "This place has brought me a great deal of happiness. I could not live anywhere else. It is such a joy to watch the budburst of vines after pruning, the growth of the shoots and leaves and then the development of the grapes." Yet such was the desperation of struggling landowners to sell when the Cullens moved into the area, their land purchases rapidly increased 20-fold, later providing the base for their highly respected vineyard and winery.

Like others, the Cullens had been enthused by WA scientist Dr John Gladstones who, in the journal of the Australian Institute of Agricultural Science in 1965, highlighted the area as extremely favourable for viticulture, given its soils and climate. He concluded that Margaret River was less prone to the extremes, like spring frosts, high temperatures in summer, and to rain or hail during the ripening period. "In many respects,"

he said, "it seemed ideal for the growing of quality grapes for wine production and looked better than Bordeaux."

Despite State Government preference in the early 1960s for wine industry diversification to go ahead at Mt Barker rather than Margaret River, medicos Tom Cullity (Vasse Felix), Kevin Cullen (Cullen Wines) and Bill Pannell (Moss Wood) moved quickly to establish their vineyards and inspire others. Among

them were the Hohnen family of Cape Mentelle who in 1983 created wine industry history by becoming the first (and still the only) WA producer to have won the coveted Royal Melbourne Wine Show Jimmy Watson Memorial Trophy for the nation's best one-year-old dry red wine.

When Cape Mentelle was successful again the following year, it removed forever any doubts about the region's ability to rival Australia's best. It must be remembered that just a few years earlier in 1977 David Hohnen's first vintage of a few hundred gallons was made in the property's tractor shed. Given such basic conditions, not even the wisest of winemen could have predicted the remarkable success that was to come, or that just a few years later in April 1990 the famous French champagne house Veuve Clicquot Ponsardin would purchase a controlling interest in Cape Mentelle.

Since then, Swiss interests have purchased Fermoy and Abbey Vale while major Australian producers Southcorp now own Devil's Lair and BRL Hardy have become joint-venture partners of Brookland Valley.

Over the years, the wines that have especially appealed include cabernet sauvignon, chardonnay, semillon, shiraz, merlot, sauvignon blanc, riesling and verdelho, while the blends of semillon sauvignon blanc and cabernet merlot are two of the nation's great industry combinations.

Among those who do it best are Amberley, Clairault, Voyager and Xanadu. But these leading producers have not just relied on wine for their reputations. They combine them with excellent cellar door facilities and eating areas, which offer the finest gourmet delights using the best local produce, to make a visit a complete experience in a great region.

Cheers to Margaret River.

AMBERLEY ESTATE

The drive into Amberley sets a scene for relaxation. One can feel problems slip away as soon as the car is parked in the shade of the majestic marri and jarrah trees and on the walk to the attractive cellar door facilities and garden restaurant. Then, sitting in comfort, the visitor can gaze out across sweeping lawns to the vines, genesis of an impressive range of premium Margaret River wines.

At the helm is Eddie Price, the son of a former currant grower from Bindoon, north of Perth. But his forte was wine rather than dried fruit and he showed his talent by becoming dux of the 1982 oenology and viticulture course at South Australia's Roseworthy College and winning their three major prizes. Then his skills were honed at the highly respected Victorian producer Brown Brothers before he returned to WA in 1989 to take up the Amberley challenge.

Two wine ranges are made: the Amberley label based only on Margaret River fruit including its own 31.5 hectare vineyard, and Charlotte Street from a selection of the best grapes the winemakers can source.

The Amberley Chardonnay,

a rich **POWERFUL** wine but with softness

and **elegance**. "This is not a wine with

a bright short life and an early death," said Price.

Shiraz at Margaret River is a region rising

star. The Amberley wine is **big and rich** with

ripe soft tannins enhanced by **spicy,**

savoury and elegant characters.

The most popular is the unpretentious Amberley Chenin Blanc. Given a dash of sauvignon blanc to provide some complexity, it is an excellent fruit-driven wine with tropical and apple flavours. A pleasant touch of residual sugar and a fresh zingy acid make it a style to please most palates as a beverage wine or with slightly spicy food or fresh fruit. Such is the chenin's appeal that it now represents half Amberley's total wine production.

Another enticing blend is the versatile, lightly oaked semillon sauvignon blanc. This dry wine is an excellent mix of grassy semillon and stone fruit flavours enhanced by ripe tropical sauvignon blanc characters.

For me, the Amberley Semillon, the estate's flagship white, has long been a favourite, ideal for example, with the restaurant's Geographe Bay filo tart. The 2001 vintage reveals more finetuning of the style especially from the early big "hero-type" wines. The vintage shows a

little more freshness and elegance and it has to be good, for it forms part of Amberley's outstanding *Semillon & Seafood Weekend*, held every February to promote the best wines from around Australia.

Export statistics show a real affinity of the English to Amberley's Sauvignon Blanc. Vineyard changes, including trellising, provide riper fruit at the tropical end of the flavour spectrum and some herbaceousness from the more shaded crop.

The biggest selling Amberley red is cabernet merlot which includes a small addition of ripe cabernet franc to add rich plummy fruit characters and weight as well as acidity. For cabernet, the northern end of Margaret River where Amberley is situated provides more of the berry characters with pleasant touches of leafy cassis and ripe tannins.

The Amberley Cabernet Sauvignon flagship red is a collector's wine. It is matured for 18 months to two years in barrel and four years in bottle before release. The philosophy behind the wine, resulting from years of planning, is to have a mature red, yet with years of cellaring life. "It is the best of the best, a few hundred cases a year and produced only in the vintages when the fruit is of the highest quality," said Price.

The new Charlotte Street label is made up of two wines, a chardonnay semillon and the unusual but striking blend of shiraz, cabernet and chardonnay. The wines were first produced in 1999. "We did it because we were looking for a fleshy, soft style of wine like Chianti," said Price. "It is not a gimmick and the wine shows that."

We have a great time making great wine and great food.

ed Margaret River Venison

Seared Margaret River Venison

Wine Match:
Amberley Cabernet Merlot –
Margaret River venison is a
consistently high quality local
product which we have
served for years. It is very
popular and this dish features
it beautifully with cabernet
merlot. The slightly sweet red
cabbage and the nutty smooth
mash match the complex fruit
flavours in the wine.

¼ large red cabbage,
shredded

60 g butter

¾ cup dark brown sugar

¼ cup red wine vinegar

salt and freshly ground
black pepper

450 g potatoes, peeled

90 g semolina, plus extra
for coating the mash cakes

50 ml cream

3 egg yolks

4 tablespoons horseradish

1 litre vegetable oil,
for frying

12 firm button mushrooms,
thinly sliced

1 litre brown veal stock
(preferably homemade)

500 ml cabernet

venison topside or beef
sirloin (allow 220 g per
serving), trimmed and
cut into 1 cm-thick slices

In a large saucepan over medium heat, cook the cabbage in the
butter until soft, add the brown sugar and vinegar, and cook until the
liquid is sticky and the cabbage is caramelised. Season with salt and
pepper. Keep warm.

In a large saucepan, cover the potatoes with cold water and bring to
the boil. Cook until soft. Drain and then mash them with the semolina,
cream, yolks, horseradish and extra salt and pepper. Cool to room
temperature. (If serving mash unfried, omit the eggs and semolina.)

To make the mash cakes: divide the mash into 4–6 cakes
approximately 3 cm thick. Coat the outside in extra semolina.
In a deep saucepan heat the oil to 180°C and deep-fry the mash
cakes until crisp and light brown. Drain on absorbent paper, and keep
warm. Then deep-fry the mushroom slices until light brown and crisp.
Drain and keep warm.

To make the cabernet jus: in a medium saucepan, bring the stock
and red wine to a steady simmer for approximately 30 minutes until
reduced to a shiny sauce (about 300ml). Keep warm.

Season the venison slices with salt and pepper. On a hot grill, sear
each side 1 minute for rare, 2 minutes for medium. Rest in warm place
for 3–5 minutes.

To serve: arrange some cabbage in the centre of each warm plate,
then spread it out to form a 15-cm diameter circle. Pour about 60 ml
jus around the outside of the cabbage. Place mash cake in the centre
of the cabbage and top with the venison. Ladle a generous
tablespoon of jus over the venison and garnish with the mushrooms.

Serves 4–6

Amberley's Geographe Bay Filo

6 filo pastry sheets

120 g melted butter

50 g (1 small) leek, washed and finely sliced

2 tablespoons flour

100 ml milk

200 ml good quality fish stock

salt and freshly ground black pepper

80 g mixed fresh herbs such as parsley, dill and chives, chopped

200 g button mushrooms, sliced

1 tablespoon pink peppercorns, washed and drained

360 g red emperor or any white-fleshed fish cut into 2 cm cubes

280 g peeled and deveined green prawns

240 g scallops, roe or coral intact

100 ml Amberley Semillon (or dry white wine)

2 tablespoons cream

1 lemon cut into wedges

fresh dill

Preheat oven to 180°C. Brush the filo sheets with half the melted butter and lay three sheets on top of each other. Cut in half across the width. Repeat with the other 3 sheets. Place in 4 greased 250 ml round bowls or tart shells, folding the edges under, and bake for about 5–10 minutes until evenly browned. Keep warm.

In a medium saucepan, sauté the leek in the remaining butter until soft. Add the flour and cook for 1–2 minutes while stirring. Slowly add the milk and stock, stirring constantly to prevent lumps forming. Simmer on low heat for 20–30 minutes, season with salt and pepper. Add the herbs, mushrooms, peppercorns and seafood. Stir in the wine and cream. Bring to a gentle simmer for 5 minutes.

Spoon the leek and seafood mixture into the filo shells, garnish with the lemon wedges and dill, and serve immediately.

Serves 4

Wine Match:
Amberley Semillon – An Amberley classic with a cult following. The toasty flavours of the pastry pair well with the oaked semillon and combine with fresh grassy overtones to balance out the sweet seafood flavours of the prawns and scallops.

Salt and Pepper Jetty Squid

Don't get too hung up about food & wine matching. It's about enjoyment.

100 ml rice wine vinegar (or white vinegar or lime/lemon juice)

1 star-anise

1 tablespoon sesame oil

50 g palm sugar (or 3 tablespoons dark brown sugar)

50 ml water

1 tablespoon salt

1 continental cucumber, sliced lengthways with a vegetable peeler, discard seeds

4 fresh squid, tentacles removed, washed and cleaned thoroughly

200 ml breadcrumbs (about 3/4 cup)

150 ml plain flour (about 2/3 cup)

2 tablespoons white pepper

1 heaped tablespoon lemon pepper

1 teaspoon crushed szechuan pepper

1 teaspoon freshly ground black pepper

1 teaspoon salt

1 1/2 litres vegetable oil, for frying

For the mayonnaise:

1 tablespoon sugar

1 small clove garlic, peeled

1/2 tablespoon salt

1 teaspoon freshly ground black pepper

1 egg

75 ml lime juice

500 ml vegetable oil

For the garnish:

shredded Asian greens (such as bok choy, tatsoi, wombok, kai lan, spinach), raw or cooked as desired

lemon or lime wedges

sprigs of fresh coriander or Vietnamese mint

In a small saucepan over high heat, bring to boil the vinegar, star-anise, sesame oil, palm sugar, water and salt. Put the cucumber strips in a mixing bowl and cover with the hot vinegar mixture. Let cool.

Slice the squid tubes lengthwise into 1cm strips. Mix the breadcrumbs, flour, peppers and salt together. Dust the squid pieces in the mix until lightly coated. Shake off any excess. Heat the oil in a deep saucepan to 180°C. Deep-fry the squid in batches until crispy and a light golden colour. Drain on absorbent paper. (If barbecuing the squid instead, omit the breadcrumbs and flour, sprinkle with the peppers and barbecue for 1–2 minutes before serving.)

To make the mayonnaise: in a food processor, blend the sugar, garlic, salt, pepper, egg and lime juice. Slowly drizzle in the vegetable oil and blend for about 4–5 minutes until thickened. Adjust seasoning if necessary. Transfer to a ramekin and keep cool.

To serve: arrange the Asian greens on a platter, top with the just-cooked squid; drain the cucumbers and arrange them with the lemon wedges and herbs around the squid. Serve immediately, with the mayonnaise on the side.

Serves 4

Chenin Granita with Summer Fruits and Macadamia Dressing

575 ml water

200 ml sugar
(about 3/4 cup)

1/2 bottle (375ml)
Amberley Chenin Blanc

70 ml lemon juice

selection of fruits such as
mango, lychee, nashi pear
or ruby grapefruit

50 ml macadamia oil
(or 150 g macadamia
nuts, toasted and crushed)

1 tablespoon caster sugar

50 ml orange juice

zest of 1 orange

1 tablespoon fresh mint,
coarsely chopped

50 g macadamia nuts,
toasted and crushed
for garnish

In a small saucepan bring 200 ml of the water and the sugar to boil for 1 minute. Transfer to a bowl, cover and leave to cool. Add the wine, the rest of the water and the lemon juice, cover and freeze, stirring every 1/2 hour until it sets into a mass of small, light crystals. Makes about 1 litre.

Wash or peel and cut 2–4 of the selected fruits into 3cm pieces. Set aside.

Put the macadamia oil, caster sugar, orange juice, zest and mint in a jar with the lid tightly on and shake together to dissolve the sugar.

Serve the granita in chilled glasses, top with chunks of fruit (2–3 of each kind), drizzle with some of the sweet dressing and garnish with the toasted nuts.

Serves 4–6

Wine Match for the Squid:
Amberley Semillon Sauvignon Blanc – This dish and the semillon sauvignon blanc are both lively, fresh and crisp. The wine has clean fruit flavours that marry well with the spices and the pickles within the dish. Overall a well balanced and flavoursome dish with a great texture combination.

Wine Match for the Granita:
Amberley Chenin Blanc – An intensely fruity, vibrant and refreshing wine, with a lovely balance of tropical aromas.

CLAIRAULT WINES

A tall lean young man is the new face of Clairault. This is Conor Martin and he represents change, dramatic change – since his family purchased the superbly sited, picturesque property at the head of Gunyulgup Creek in 1999. Their impact has taken the small low-profile producer to become a major state player, a 1000-tonnes-per-annum-plus producer.

Bill and Ena Martin had been coming to Margaret River for over 20 years, attracted to the area because it reminded them in many ways of their home in Ireland. Before they took up the challenge of owning a vineyard and winery, Clairault had been established with its first plantings in 1976 and was well regarded for its premium wines. It was originally named after Cape Clairault, a headland on the nearby coast that is a prominent local landmark to the south of the popular surfing beach at Yallingup.

The Martin changes have seen major winery, storage and warehouse area extensions and a completely refurbished and extended alfresco dining area built around a shady giant marri tree. From there, visitors can take in the sweeping landscaped gardens and vineyard views as part of an expanded cellar door tasting facility, or simply relax on the deck sampling the latest releases that make perfect partners for the many innovative dishes on Clairault's menu.

"We pick all our fruit in small batches at different ripeness levels. This allows a **wide range of flavours** to emerge in the final blends, which change and develop with time in the bottle, adding to the overall complexity and **ENJOYMENT** of each glass."

– Winemaker Peter Stark

The stand-alone reserve red says **QUALITY** from the first sniff. This rich but refined blend of cabernet (the main variety) merlot and cabernet franc sells for around $50 a bottle, which makes it a **special occasion wine** well worth the money.

Among the vines, another Martin son Brian has been busy helping viticulturist Nick Macpherson expand the plantings that will see a swing from white variety domination to reds. Their environmentally responsible, low intervention approach to the growing of wine grapes includes the use of guinea fowl, allowed to roam free to eat the majority of weevils and crickets that sometimes appear.

Winemaker Peter Stark is dedicated to creating a range of elegant wines that show exceptional balance, structure and individuality. He and executive chef Andrea Ilott, who runs a seasonal menu, have been struggling to keep up with demand, such has been the rapidly increasing visitor numbers keen to sip the wine range and to sample the tasty dishes on offer.

Eventually, 80 hectares of the 125 hectare property will be graced by

vines though fruit purchases will continue from selected contract growers in the Margaret River area. Conor says to cater for the growth, a new winery is planned by 2004 allowing for wine tastings to be transferred to the original winery away from the restaurant.

A feature of Clairault is that it has three creeks and a permanent forest soak used extensively last century by weary travellers on the journey from Bunbury to Augusta. This earthy Australiana reflection provided the inspiration for the latest flavoursome wine range, Swagman's Kiss. In 2001, a chardonnay was added to the premium dry white blend of sauvignon blanc, semillon and chardonnay. The Bordeaux-blend red is made up of cabernet, cabernet franc and merlot. A shiraz is planned for 2002.

The flagship Clairault range, which included a riesling and cabernet sauvignon in 2001 for the first time, is impressive. It also has a sauvignon blanc (one of my favourites from the region), semillon sauvignon blanc, cabernet merlot, reserve cabernet and a delicious, decadent, luscious-style, late-harvest wine, fortified-with-aged brandy. A merlot is planned for 2002.

Clairault's natural advantages include its elevation – 120 metres above sea level, higher than most in the state – and the Gunyulgup Creek, which runs down to Smiths Beach, allowing for moderating cool winds from the sea to flow to the highest part of the property, helping extend ripening periods for better balanced fruit.

ccan Sweet Potato and Charred Corn Soup with Dukkah

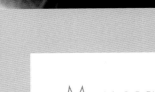

Wine Match for the Soup:
Clairault Semillon Sauvignon Blanc – Attractive lemon blossom, a hint of spice and a faint herbal edge in this wine bring out the best of the soup's creamy sweet potato and yoghurt texture, which is offset by the crunchiness of the hazelnut and eastern spices. A marriage made in heaven!

Wine Match for Osso Bucco:
1999 Clairault Cabernet Merlot – The persistence, harmony and fruit intensity are clear indicators of the cabernet merlot's quality. The soft, fleshy fruit with juicy plum and cherry flavours, offset by a fine tannin grip and nicely handled oak, provide exceptional balance to the intense rich tomato, red wine, lemon parsley and olive oil flavours of the osso bucco.

Moroccan Sweet Potato and Charred Corn Soup with Dukkah

70 ml olive oil

1 large brown onion, diced

2 cloves garlic, crushed

1 teaspoon ground cinnamon

1 teaspoon ground ginger

1 teaspoon ground cumin

1 teaspoon ground coriander

1/2 teaspoon chilli powder

2 1/2 litres chicken or vegetable stock

2 teaspoons sugar

juice of 1 lemon

1 bay leaf

salt and freshly ground black pepper

1 1/2 kg or 3 large sweet potatoes, peeled and diced

2 corn cobs

For the dukkah:

50 g hazelnuts

4 tablespoons sesame seeds

2 tablespoons coriander seeds

2 tablespoons cumin seeds

1 teaspoon salt

1/2 teaspoon freshly ground black pepper

1/2 teaspoon sugar

For the garnish:

1/3 cup natural yoghurt

1 tablespoon fresh coriander, chopped

1 tablespoon fresh mint, chopped

Heat the olive oil in a large saucepan and gently cook the onion and garlic until they soften. Add the spices and cook for a minute or so, stirring constantly to avoid burning. Add the rest of the ingredients except the corn and simmer until the sweet potato is soft.

Remove the bay leaf, cool the mixture slightly then puree in a food processor or with a hand blender.

Grill the corn cobs over a gas flame or bake in a hot (200°C) oven to char slightly. Cut off the corn kernels and stir them into the soup.

To make the dukkah: roast the hazelnuts, sesame, coriander and cumin seeds in a preheated 180°C oven until lightly browned. Place them in a food processor with the salt, pepper and sugar and blend briefly to a crumbly mixture. Be careful not to over blend as it will turn into a paste very quickly. (Dukkah will keep in an airtight container in the fridge for a couple of weeks and is also great with bread and good-quality olive oil as a dip.)

To serve: adjust the seasoning, bring the soup back to the boil and serve hot. Garnish with a spoonful of yoghurt, chopped herbs and dukkah on top.

Serves 6

Veal Osso Bucco with Sugar-Crusted Parsnips and Beetroot Gremolata

6 thick or 12 smaller pieces veal shin

1 cup flour

salt and freshly ground black pepper

70 g butter

3 tablespoons olive oil

2 cups (500ml) dry red wine

1 onion, finely chopped

1 bay leaf

500 g tomatoes, peeled, seeded and chopped

2 teaspoons brown sugar

3 teaspoons balsamic vinegar

1 tablespoon tomato paste

1 1/2 litres beef stock

For the parsnips:

6 medium parsnips, peeled and topped

2 tablespoons olive oil

2 teaspoon caster sugar

1/2 teaspoon crushed garlic

salt and freshly ground black pepper

For the gremolata:

2 medium beetroots, roasted or boiled

2 tablespoons flat-leaf parsley, coarsely chopped

zest and juice of 1 lemon

1 clove garlic, very finely sliced

1 1/4 tablespoons extra-virgin olive oil

shaved parmesan for garnish

Preheat the oven to 180°C. Roll the veal in the seasoned flour. In a large frypan, heat the butter and olive oil and cook the veal until just browned. Place in an ovenproof dish, add the wine and rest of the ingredients. Cover the dish with a lid or alfoil and bake in the oven for 45 minutes, checking occasionally to see that the meat is still covered with liquid. If not, add more stock and cook for another 45 minutes. The sauce should be thick and the meat quite tender. If it is not tender, cook for a further 20 minutes.

Tie the thin ends of the parsnips together with an elastic band or string and place them bottoms down in a saucepan with enough cold water to cover the thick parts. Bring to the boil and simmer until soft, about 8 minutes. Drain. Mix the olive oil, sugar, garlic and seasoning and coat the parsnips. Lay them flat in a roasting pan and cook in a preheated 200°C oven for 20 minutes or until crisp.

To make the gremolata: peel and dice the beetroot into a bowl. Mix in the other ingredients. Add seasoning if desired. Set aside.

To serve: ladle a piece of veal osso bucco into a bowl (with potato mash, if desired); arrange a parsnip on top and sprinkle with parmesan and freshly ground pepper. Serve the gremolata on the side to finish. (This dish can be made 1 or 2 days ahead to develop the flavours.)

Serves 6

We create each dish using only the freshest & best ingredients to marry perfectly with our elegant wines.

Spaghetti with Feta, Almonds, Lemon and Oregano

750 g spaghetti or similar pasta (preferably handmade)

300 ml good quality olive oil

3 cloves garlic, crushed

150 g almond kernels, slightly bashed

juice and zest of 2 lemons

150 ml Clairault Semillon Sauvignon Blanc (or a good quality white wine)

8 medium tomatoes, peeled, seeded and chopped

200 g feta cheese, cut into small cubes

3 tablespoons fresh oregano leaves, chopped

salt and freshly ground black pepper

shaved parmesan for garnish

Bring a large saucepan of salted water to the boil and cook the pasta to *al dente*.

In a deep saucepan, warm the olive oil and garlic. Add the almonds, lemon juice, zest and wine. Simmer for a few minutes to reduce the liquid slightly. Add the tomatoes, feta and oregano. Turn off the heat, stir in the pasta to coat well with the oil, and adjust seasoning. Be careful not to add too much salt as some feta can be very salty.

Serve with freshly ground black pepper and shaved parmesan. (This dish is also good with grilled squid, sliced chillies or sun-dried tomatoes.)

Serves 6

SWAGMAN'S KISS

Chardonnay
MARGARET RIVER
750mL

Wine Match:
Clairault Swagman's Kiss Chardonnay – This wine bursts with peach and melon flavours, balanced by delicious buttery notes and an underlying acidity that ensures each sip is fresh and lively – not unlike this dish! A very enjoyable combination of flavours that is clean, precise and lingering on the palate.

Berry Brulee and Jelly with Boysenberry Sorbet

750 ml cream

6 egg yolks

1/3 cup caster sugar

1 vanilla bean (or 1/2 teaspoon essence)

1 cinnamon stick (or 1/2 teaspoon ground cinnamon)

2 cups of raspberries, blueberries, mulberries or strawberries

For the berry jelly:

600 ml water

1/4 cup caster sugar

2 berry flavoured tea bags (we use Twinings strawberry and mango)

2 gelatine leaves, softened in cold water

The sorbet:

boysenberry sorbet (preferably Simmo's from Dunsborough)

In a large saucepan over medium heat, bring the cream to the boil. In a heatproof bowl, combine the yolks, the sugar, vanilla and cinnamon. Whisk in the hot cream and return the entire mixture to the saucepan. Stir continuously on low heat until the custard thickens to coat the back of the spoon (about 8–10 minutes). Be careful not to overcook or it will scramble.

Place the saucepan in a sink of cold water to cool. Discard the vanilla bean and cinnamon stick.

Divide half the berries into 6 espresso cups or small ramekins then pour in the cooled custard. Chill overnight. Sprinkle a little caster sugar on top and place under a hot grill for about 10 minutes to form a hard toffee crust.

To make the jelly: bring the water to the boil in a saucepan, add the sugar. When the sugar has dissolved remove the pan from the heat. Add the tea bags and infuse for 5 minutes. Remove the tea bags. Add the gelatine leaves to the hot tea mix, and gently stir until they are completely dissolved. Pour into 6 shot glasses or small ramekins, (leaving room for the other half of the berries). Cool to room temperature then float the berries on the top. Chill for at least 3 hours to set.

To serve: place everything together on a big plate and serve with a scoop of sorbet on the side. Great as a light alternative for Christmas lunch. (This recipe is best made a day in advance so that everything can set!)

Serves 6

Wine Match:
Clairault Alexis Port – Rich ripe red fruits with prune and blackcurrant complement the berry sensations in the dessert.

VOYAGER ESTATE

A bicycle ride from Canada to Mexico gave Cliff Royle lots of time to think, as well as take in the sights. Finally on the long journey, the young man resolved to give away a planned career in finance and management and turn to the science of wine. But he could never have imagined on that cycling marathon that the decision was to lead in a few short years to senior winemaker at Voyager Estate.

One of Margaret River's premium producers, it is a striking centre for visitors with its distinctive Cape Dutch architecture and magnificent garden landscaping. Previously, Cliff Royle had studied business at Western Australia's Curtin University, but while working in a Melbourne hotel and bottle shop he had been urged by winemaking friends Stuart Pym and Janice McDonald to take up winemaking studies at Charles Sturt University.

Later, in 1997, Pym employed Royle as his assistant at Voyager, and when he moved on, principal Michael Wright put Royle in charge. It was a daunting challenge, for the decade of the 1990s had seen Voyager wines reach new levels of refinement and sophistication. The initial Royle vintage was in 2000 – some 20 000 cases from the estate's 73 hectares of carefully tended vineyards, increasing to almost 25 000 cases the following year.

Top of the range are the limited production **classical**

Tom Price reserve duo – a barrel-selected red in only the

best vintage years and a sauvignon blanc semillon blend

that is aged for a year in new **FRENCH OAK**

and kept in bottle for three years before release.

Chardonnay and cabernet merlot make up the

next tier followed by semillon, shiraz and sauvignon blanc semillon

and then chenin – a wine range **likened** by Voyager to

FRENCH WINES rated Grand Cru, Premier

Cru and Villages.

To ensure the strictest quality control, fruit is no longer purchased from outside sources. Perhaps that move in itself reflects Michael Wright's dedication to quality in everything Voyager represents, be it a rose in the glorious garden or a ripening bunch of grapes among Voyager's thousands of vines. His entry into the industry in 1991 was a dramatic alternative to family involvement in the state's Pilbara iron ore industry. But he has embraced the direction with relish, leaving no stone unturned in the ultimate search for quality.

That is equally evident in the solid-walled entrance gates leading to the hilltop facility with its sweeping views of row upon row of vines among the rolling hills, as it is in the wines themselves.

While neighbouring icon Leeuwin Estate has set national benchmarks for its chardonnay, the carefully made Voyager wines of the variety have been proud West Australian products. Over the years, complexity

and texture have been enhanced with layers of flavour like green honeydew melons and pink grapefruit combined with the skilful use of oak – excellent with white meats and seafood, especially salmon.

The classy Voyager Estate Cabernet Merlots, which include a small amount of cabernet franc and petit verdot, are matured in French oak for two years. To avoid green, eucalypt characters, recent years have seen Voyager pushing the boundaries on fruit ripeness in the quest for richer cassis, darker chocolate flavours though retaining hints of mint, certainly achieved in the 1998 and 1999 vintages.

The most popular Voyager wine is the sauvignon blanc semillon, a lightly oaked joyous blend of fruit flavours with a lovely clean, fresh acid finish, as in the excellent 2000 wine. Underlying the passionfruit and gooseberry from the sauvignon blanc which made up 55 per cent of the blend, is the semillon that provides pleasant levels of herbaceous characters. Delicious is the word for this wine that can be enjoyed as a beverage style or with a range of appetisers.

Voyager also produces a cellar door special, a non-alcoholic sparkling grape juice made from semillon and chenin. And it has to be good as it caters for the taste of Michael Wright who is a teetotaller.

Voyager is different, attracting many for its uniqueness. In this way, Margaret River as a whole benefits.

onut Crusted Chicken

Wine Match for the Chicken:
Voyager Estate Chardonnay –
For this dish of contrasting
flavours, a refined well-
weighted wine is required.
With fine balance and length,
beautiful toasty French oak,
enveloping grapefruit, white
peach and melon, this
chardonnay is such a wine.

Wine Match for the Marron:
Voyager Estate Sauvignon
Blanc Semillon – A perfect
balance of zesty citrus fruits
and gooseberries combined
with a crisp persistent
acidity and lingering finish
makes this wine the perfect
complement to the mineral-
sweet quality of the marron,
the peppery rocket, the sweet
capsicum and sharpness of the
parmesan and mustard.

Coconut Crusted Chicken

12 chicken thighs (preferably Mount
Barker free-range), skinned and boned

2 tablespoons tamarind paste

1/2 cup olive oil

2 cloves garlic, finely chopped

salt and freshly ground black pepper

3 heads garlic,
peeled and sliced

75 g fresh ginger, chopped

12 spring onions, sliced

1/4 cup fresh coriander leaves

50 ml vegetable oil

50 ml light soy sauce

1 large red capsicum

1 large yellow capsicum

50 g butter

1 large onion, finely chopped

100 ml Voyager Estate Chardonnay

400 ml chicken stock

400 ml pouring cream

300 ml coconut cream

400 g coconut milk powder

30 snow peas

12 slices crusty bread

50 g fresh basil plus
extra sprigs for garnish

Place the chicken thighs in a bowl. Add the tamarind paste, half
the olive oil, the garlic and seasoning. Mix thoroughly, cover and
refrigerate for 2 hours, turning occasionally.

In a food processor, blend the heads of garlic, ginger, spring
onions and coriander to a rough paste. With the motor running,
slowly add the vegetable oil and soy sauce until smooth. (This
relish can be refrigerated in a sealed jar for up to 3 days.)

Slice the capsicums into thirds and deseed. Flatten each piece on
a cutting board and remove and chop the inner flesh. Set aside
the outer skins. In a saucepan over medium heat, melt the butter,
add the chopped onion and sauté until soft. Add the wine, chicken
stock and pouring cream. Bring to the boil and then simmer until
the liquid is reduced by half. Stir in the capsicum flesh and coconut
cream. To thicken the sauce, add half the coconut milk powder.
Season to taste. Keep warm.

Slice the capsicum skins into fine juliennes and place them in a
bowl of ice water to curl. Slice the snow peas thinly and place in
a bowl of cold water.

In a food processor, blend the bread to rough crumbs. Add the rest
of the olive oil, the rest of the coconut milk powder and the basil
and mix well. In a lightly oiled frypan fry the chicken for about
3–4 minutes on each side until almost cooked. Remove to a
grilling tray. Cover each chicken piece with a generous amount
of the coconut mix. Grill under medium heat until golden brown.

To serve: spoon some coconut sauce in the centre of 6 dinner
plates. Place a mound of snow peas over the sauce. Arrange the
chicken on top and garnish with the curly capsicum, a sprig of
basil and a teaspoon of the relish on the side.

Serves 6

Margaret River Marron Salad

18 medium-sized marron tails

200 g butter

juice and grated zest of 1 lime

salt and freshly ground black pepper

2 medium yellow capsicums

60 ml white vinegar

3 egg yolks

60 g Dijon mustard

330 ml olive oil

100 g sliced white bread, cut into small cubes for croutons

3 mangoes

300 g rocket, washed, stems removed and refrigerated to keep crisp

60 g shaved parmesan

sprigs bronze fennel and 3 limes, halved, for garnish

Butterfly the marron tails by cutting in half lengthwise. In a food processor, blend the butter, lime juice and zest, and salt and pepper to a smooth paste. Smear over the marron flesh and set aside.

Slice the capsicum into thirds and deseed. Flatten each piece on a cutting board and remove the inner flesh. Set aside the outer skins. In a saucepan over medium heat cook the capsicum flesh in the vinegar until tender (about 7 minutes). Allow to cool. Blend the mixture in a food processor then add the egg yolks and mustard. While blending, slowly add 300 ml of the olive oil until the liquid thickens.

Slice the capsicum skins into fine julienne strips. Place in ice water to curl.

To make the croutons: heat the oven to 180°C, place the bread cubes on a baking tray and drizzle with the remaining 30 ml olive oil. Bake until golden (about 10 minutes).

Peel the mangoes, cut a slice off each side and cut the 6 slices in half lengthwise. In a saucepan over high heat, quickly sauté the pieces in a dab of butter to brown lightly. Set aside.

On a hot grill or barbecue, cook the marron tails for 10 minutes until all the flesh is cooked (opaque in colour).

To serve: arrange the rocket onto plates and drizzle with the dressing. Top with the mango, grilled marron, croutons and parmesan. Garnish with the capsicum, lime and fennel.

Serves 6

Field Mushrooms Filled with Pine Nuts and Basil Bread Crust

2 medium eggplants

50 ml olive oil

1/2 medium onion, finely chopped

50 g butter

200 ml Voyager Estate Sauvignon Blanc Semillon

20 ml tarragon vinegar

400 ml tomato juice

2 tablespoons fresh tarragon, roughly chopped

8 thick slices crusty bread

2 tablespoons fresh basil

30 g pine nuts

salt and freshly ground black pepper

6 medium to large field mushrooms, stems removed

Dijon mustard

6 Kytren goat's cheese discs (about 300 g total)

Cut the eggplants into 1 1/2 cm thick slices. Dust with salt and leave for 30 minutes in a colander in the sink to drain off the bitter juices. Rinse off the salt and place on a cloth to dry. Drizzle half the olive oil over the slices. Char-grill the slices over a hot grill or barbecue for 3 minutes on each side. Keep warm.

In a medium saucepan, sauté the onion in the butter until soft. Add the wine, vinegar and tomato juice and simmer until reduced by one third. Add salt and pepper to taste. Add the chopped tarragon and simmer for a further 5 minutes. Keep warm.

In a food processor, blend the bread, basil, pine nuts, salt and pepper. Slowly add the remaining olive oil to moisten.

Preheat the oven to 200°C. Place the mushrooms on a baking tray and brush the inner caps with Dijon mustard. Fill the caps with enough bread crust mixture to create a small mound. Slice the goat's cheese pieces into quarters and arrange on top. Bake the mushrooms for about 12 minutes, then put them under the grill for about 1–2 minutes to ensure the crust is golden brown.

Spoon the sauce on to 6 dinner plates. Arrange the eggplant slices on the sauce and top with the mushrooms. Garnish with a crisp sprig of tarragon or basil.

Serves 6

At Voyager Estate restaurant creating a synergy between food and wine influences all that we do.

Fig and Ginger Pudding

500 ml water

340 g dried figs, diced

1 teaspoon vanilla essence

1 teaspoon bicarbonate of soda

120 g butter

340 g brown sugar

4 eggs, lightly beaten

350 g self-raising flour, sifted

150 g glacé ginger, chopped

In a large saucepan, bring the water, figs, vanilla and bicarbonate of soda to boil for 5 minutes. Remove from the heat and cool slightly, then add the butter and brown sugar. Add the eggs and fold in the flour and ginger.

Preheat the oven to 180°C. Pour the mixture into 12 greased and floured 200 ml round pudding moulds. Bake for 30 minutes. Serve immediately. (Goes well with caramel sauce and vanilla bean ice cream. The puddings can be made in advance, then reheated in the microwave.)

Serves 12

Wine Match for the Mushrooms: Voyager Estate Cabernet Sauvignon Merlot 1997 – The firm texture and forest floor earthiness of the mushrooms, with the subdued creamy pungency of goat's cheese and the leafy freshness of the herbs, all work beautifully with the merlot. With its full body, layers of black forest fruits, balanced with fine, integrated, chalky tannins and lingering cedar oaks, look no further for a perfect wine match.

Wine Match for the Pudding: A rich luscious dessert wine or Tokay.

XANADU

A new entrance into Xanadu is more than just a driveway. It is a statement of change. For the new "front door" represents a new era as the family-owned wine producer became a publicly listed company. Founding doctors John Lagan and wife Eithne Sheridan purchased the 160-hectare property just 4 km from Margaret River in 1970, planting the first vines seven years later. Subsequently, son Conor was given the management challenge.

In April 2001, the family decided to accept an offer for their operation. Chateau Xanadu then became Xanadu Wines Pty Ltd and was listed on the Australian Stock Exchange. This meant that for the first time, the founders had outside shareholders. It also meant that vital development capital was available to take Xanadu forward.

The transformation was swift and included a new 135-hectare block at Karridale, called *Jindawarra*, for vineyard expansion, winery upgrade and extension to 2500-tonne capacity, a café-style restaurant, barbecue area and children's playground, as well as the conversion of the warehouse storage area into an art gallery. Within two years, a young, vibrant management team led by Andrew Moore, has achieved sales of 55 000 cases with plans for a further 100 000 within the next five years. Production at the time of purchase was just 12 000 cases.

Since my first sip of a Xanadu Semillon in 1985, I have had a soft spot for the wine, especially with seafood. The **QUALITY** of fruit and its balance makes it a real alternative to chardonnay and I have **rated highly** recent vintages.

Extensive plantings of merlot indicate Xanadu's faith in the **rich, soft, plummy** variety. The impressive 1999 vintage brought further honours to Western Australia with a **GOLD MEDAL** at New York's 2001 Intervin competition.

Curiously, Jurg Muggli, responsible for the vines and wines of Xanadu, is a man who initially trained and worked as a chef in his native Switzerland before turning to viticulture and oenology studies. Friendship with a young Australian workmate during his involvement with vineyards around Zurich and making wine for several producers, led to migration and a job with respected Hunter Valley producer Brokenwood. In 1990 he met Conor who offered him a job for "a couple of weeks". Soon he was entrenched, introducing European ideas and organic growing practices to his new environment.

Top wine of the Xanadu range is the limited-release Lagan Estate Cabernet Reserve, a super premium blend of cabernet sauvignon, cabernet franc and merlot. Selling for around $60 a bottle, it is made from the old original vine plantings, a "golden resource" according to Conor. Rich and intense with great smoothness and length, it is a wine to sip and savour for the joys of fruit and oak that swamp the palate.

The premium range under the Xanadu label includes a chardonnay, semillon, riesling, (from Frankland River fruit) semillon sauvignon blanc, noble semillon, shiraz, cabernet and merlot.

So good was the 1998 Xanadu Chardonnay that in 2000, it beat almost 8000 other Australian wines to win the coveted Australian Wine and Brandy Corporation's George Mackey Trophy for the nation's best export wine. This was followed by the 2000 vintage winning a gold medal at the 2001 London International Wine Challenge.

Xanadu's third label, the early-drinking Secession, is based on fruit from around WA and is Xanadu's equivalent to the Margaret River classics. Included are a red and white blend that may change each year, depending on fruit availability and quality. Such was the standard of the 2000 Shiraz Cabernet (export) that it too won gold at the London Challenge.

Finally, Xanadu has continued its award-winning success, claiming gold medals for both their 1998 Lagan Estate Cabernet Reserve and 1999 Xanadu Cabernet Sauvignon at the 2001 Intervin Wine Competition in New York.

So the dragon emblem introduced to the label design in the 1990s marches on, as a strong stamp of authority as well as of the modern Xanadu.

A fantastic food and wine match that is a refreshing start to a meal.

Grilled Chilli and Lemon Grass Prawns

Wine Match for the Prawns:
2001 Xanadu Riesling –
The classic riesling characters
of fragrant citrus and minerals
combine perfectly with Asian
inspired dishes incorporating
lime, coriander, chilli and
lemon grass.

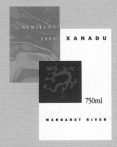

Wine Match for the Chicken:
2000 Xanadu Semillon –
Vine leaves impart a natural
lemon flavour into food, which
is so compatible with the lemon
zestiness and spice found in the
2000 Semillon.

Grilled Chilli and Lemon Grass Prawns

18 large green prawn cutlets
(if using whole prawns, remove
the head and shell but leave
the tail intact)

9 lemon grass stalks,
tough outer layers removed
(6 to be used as skewers)

2 large red chillies,
seeded and chopped

2 teaspoons grated fresh ginger

1 cup plus 2 tablespoons fresh
coriander, coarsely
chopped or torn

5 tablespoons lime juice

2 tablespoons peanut oil

200 g bean thread (or
cellophane) noodles

1/2 cup mint leaves,
coarsely chopped

2 tablespoons fish sauce

2 tablespoons
Thai sweet chilli sauce

1 cup fresh jackfruit or
fresh mango pieces

1 lime, cut into six
wedges for garnish

Remove intestinal vein from the prawns and thread 3 prawns on
to each of the 6 trimmed lemon grass skewers.

Finely chop the remaining lemon grass. In a bowl, combine the
lemon grass with the chillies, ginger, 2 tablespoons of the coriander,
2 tablespoons of the lime juice and the peanut oil. Pour this over the
skewered prawns, cover and refrigerate for 1–2 hours, turning the
prawns occasionally in the marinade.

In a bowl, cover the noodles with boiling water and let stand for
3 minutes or until soft, then drain well. Combine the noodles with
the remaining herbs, the fish sauce, the rest of the lime juice, the chilli
sauce and the jackfruit or mango.

Cook the prawns over a hot grill or barbecue for 1–2 minutes each
side or until they change colour.

Mound a little salad on to each plate, top with the skewered prawns
and serve with a wedge of lime on the side.

Serves 6

Chicken Wrapped in Vine Leaves with Goat's Cheese and Escalibada Salad

250 g small Japanese eggplants

2 red capsicums

2 medium red onions, peeled

6 Roma vine-ripened tomatoes, quartered

6 artichoke hearts cooked and halved (if unable to obtain fresh, use tinned)

200 ml olive oil

3 tablespoons lemon juice

2 cloves garlic, crushed

1 tablespoon chopped flat-leaf parsley

1 teaspoon baby capers

salt and freshly ground black pepper

6 x 200 g chicken breasts (preferably free range), trimmed and skin removed

6 slices firm goat's cheese

6 vine leaves (preferably fresh leaves that have been thoroughly washed then blanched in boiling water. If using the tinned, brined variety, thoroughly soak and rinse before using)

To make the escalibada salad: preheat the oven to 190°C. In a lightly oiled roasting pan place the eggplants, capsicums and onions, and bake for about 30 minutes turning occasionally. (The onions will still be slightly crunchy; the eggplants and capsicums should be wrinkled and slightly browned.) Peel the eggplants and capsicums, deseed the capsicums, and cut them all into 1-cm strips. Slice the onions lengthways. Place the lot in a bowl with the fresh tomatoes and artichoke hearts. Set aside.

In a small bowl, whisk together 100 ml of the olive oil, the lemon juice, garlic, parsley, capers and salt and pepper to taste. Pour into the vegetable mixture, mix gently and chill to amalgamate the flavours. Bring to just under room temperature when ready to serve.

Season both sides of the chicken with salt and pepper. Place a slice of the cheese on top of each breast and wrap a vine leaf over, folding the leaf under the chicken.

In a deep frypan, heat the remaining olive oil over medium heat and fry the wrapped chicken, first on the side with vine leaf edges wrapped under, for 4–5 minutes which will help seal the chicken and prevent the goat's cheese from melting too early. Then gently turn the chicken over and cook the other side until tender (about 4 minutes).

Serve the chicken on a bed of the escalibada salad and garnish with fresh basil or parsley.

Serves 6

Sashimi of Tasmanian Salmon with Asian Slaw

1 clove garlic, sliced

1 small knob fresh ginger, finely chopped

1 tablespoon fish sauce

100 ml lime juice

50 ml rice wine vinegar

75 g palm sugar, grated or crushed

1/4 small bok choy, outer leaves removed, finely shredded

1 medium carrot, peeled and julienned

1 medium red onion, finely chopped

1/2 continental cucumber, peeled, seeded and sliced lengthways with a vegetable peeler

100 g fresh bean sprouts

1 hot red chilli, seeded and julienned

1/4 cup Vietnamese hot (or regular) mint leaves, coarsely chopped

1/4 cup basil leaves, coarsely chopped or torn

1/2 cup coriander leaves, coarsely chopped

100 g toasted peanuts, roughly chopped

600 g Sashimi-quality Tasmanian salmon, taken from the fillet and sliced thinly

To make the dressing: shake the first six ingredients together, in a jar with the lid firmly on, until the sugar is dissolved. (Any excess dressing will keep in this airtight container in the fridge for 1–2 weeks.)

Mix together the bok choy, carrot, onion, cucumber and bean sprouts in a large bowl. Add the chilli (more if you like it hot) and herbs, and then stir enough dressing through the salad to moisten. Scatter with the peanuts.

Assemble with the sliced salmon on top.

Serves 6

Quality steak, silky mash and a well made jus are the keys to this dish.

Aged Beef Rib Eye with Garlic Mash, Carrot Chips and Roasted Shallot Jus

500 g potatoes, peeled and cut in half

5 cloves garlic, peeled

150 g butter

150 ml olive oil

200 ml cream (or milk, if desired)

sea salt and freshly ground black pepper

30 shallots or small white pickling onions

2 litres vegetable oil for deep-frying

2 carrots, peeled and sliced thinly with a vegetable peeler

fresh green vegetables such as beans, Asian greens, broccolini, asparagus

600 ml good quality reduced red wine beef stock (jus)

6 aged rib eye steaks, on the bone

Place the potatoes and garlic into a saucepan of cold salted water, bring to the boil and simmer gently until potatoes are soft. Drain thoroughly. Mash the potatoes using a potato masher or mouli (do not use a food processor as the result will be potato glue). Add the butter and 70 ml of the olive oil. Warm the cream and add as necessary, depending on the starchiness of potatoes, to achieve a silky smooth texture. Add seasoning to taste. (The mash can be made in advance and heated through with a little extra milk or cream.)

Preheat the oven to 160°C. Toss the shallots with the remaining olive oil and roast on a tray for about 50 minutes until soft. Squeeze the shallots from their skins, discard the skins.

Heat the oil in a deep saucepan to 150°C. Fry the carrot chips in batches until they look crisp (about 4 minutes). They actually crisp further once removed from the pan. Drain on absorbent paper. (The chips will keep for 2 days in an airtight container at room temperature.) The oil can be strained and reused as frying oil.

Cook the green vegetables as desired: blanched beans tossed in butter, grilled garlicky asparagus or broccolini tossed in the wok. Gently reheat the shallots in the jus.

On a hot grill or barbecue, grill the beef ribs to medium rare (6–8 minutes on each side) turning only once. Season with salt and pepper. Cover with alfoil and leave for 15 minutes in a warm place.

To serve: pile a generous dollop of heated garlic mash on a warm plate. Rest the beef rib at an angle against the mash, sit the green vegetables on the other side, pour the red wine jus around the plate and finish with a teepee of carrot chips on top.

Serves 6

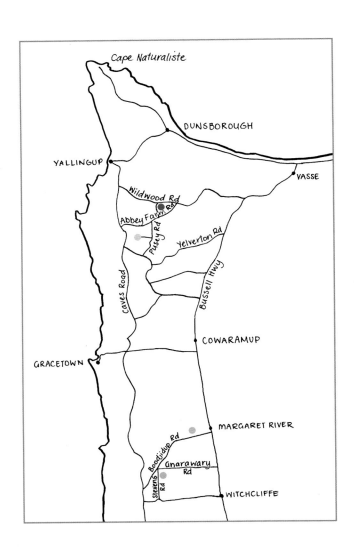

● **Amberley Estate**
Cnr Thornton and Wildwood Roads, Yallingup
Cellar door sales: daily 10am–4.30pm
Restaurant: daily 10.30am–4pm; Sat. 6pm–9pm
Tel: 08 9755 2288
Fax: 08 9755 2171

● **Clairault Wines**
Henry Road (off Pusey Road), Willyabrup
Cellar door sales and restaurant: daily 10am–5pm
Tel: 08 9755 6225
Reservations: 08 9755 6655
Fax: 08 9755 6229

● **Voyager Estate**
Stevens Road (off Gnarawary Road), Margaret River
Cellar door sales and restaurant: daily 10am–5pm
Tel: 08 9757 6354
Fax: 08 9757 6494

● **Xanadu**
Boodjidup Road, Margaret River
Cellar door sales and restaurant/bbq: daily 10am–5pm
Tel: 08 9757 2581
Fax: 08 9757 3389